GW00497039

LITTLE BOOK OF
CRIME &
PUNISHMENT

Michelle Brachet

LITTLE BOOK OF

CRIME &
PUNISHMENT

First published in the UK in 2012

© Demand Media Limited 2012

www.demand-media.co.uk

Printed and bound in China

ISBN 978-1-909217-24-9

The views in this book are those of the author but they are general
views only and readers are urged to consult the relevant and
qualified specialist for individual advice in particular situations.

Contents

Introduction

We live in a society where every aspect of our everyday lives is governed by the law. We are subject to rules and regulations from where we can walk, and where we can't, how we are allowed to behave in public, what we are allowed to even say in public, and when and how much we can consume alcohol. No one is above the law; it affects the rich and poor, the famous, the homeless, the leaders, the politicians and the monarchy.

The law we live with today has been 2,000 years in the making and it is still a work in progress. The assumption cannot be made that laws will always change for the better, but if we have a better understanding of where the law today came from, we can keep a better eye on where it is going.

The story and journey of the development of our laws over time is both fascinating and sometimes bizarre. Somehow we have moved from the times of trial by boiling water, through decapitation and hanging, to the emergence of court room trials as we know our modern democracy to be today.

Beginning with the Normans and how they created the very first surveillance society, followed by the very beginnings of our often ludicrous compensation culture thanks to the Anglo-Saxons, we move to banging people up instead of stringing people up following a story that involves a man whose body was kept in a London

cupboard. Strange perhaps, fascinating definitely and frighteningly all true, some of the circumstances, the result of which we are all now governed by as our modern law developed, may surprise even the most liberal of minds.

The first part of this book looks at the last 2,000 years of British history and how events of the past have had an effect on the development of our legal system as we know it today.

The second part takes a closer look at several historical events mentioned in more detail: the reign of Queen Mary I, known notoriously as 'Bloody Mary'; the Witchfinder General; and the Monmouth Rebellion, the result of which saw hundreds of hangings carried out in just a few days. Of course, there are many more historically fundamental events in our history that have had a serious influence on the course our country has taken in the last 2,000 years, but it is hoped the subjects covered here give the reader an interesting and fascinating snapshot into the past.

What a Bloody Feud!

The history of our law is intrinsically linked to our country's geography. Due to the fact that we are a nation on an island, we have been subject to wave after wave of invaders for centuries. Every time this has happened, the invaders have had an influence on the direction our nation has subsequently taken, as they have all had their own way of doing things.

The 1st millennium A.D. saw our nation deal with four invasions and a conquest, beginning with the Romans and ending with the Normans. The very foundations of English law were laid over these years and are paramount to the development of the legal system, as we know it today.

The Romans were the first to invade. They have always had a reputation for having built the greatest empire the world had ever seen, and they imposed their culture on everyone and everything wherever they went. The Romans are renowned for amazing architecture, great public buildings, straight roads, heated baths, drainage systems, art, literature, education; there isn't much the Romans are not famous for, in fact. In terms of law and order, however, the Romans fell some way short of the mark in leaving their stamp in this regard.

There are three very large books of Roman law – the Novellae, the Codex, and the Digest. They are, however, all for a period long after the Romans left Britain. There is not a trace of the law the Romans used while they were in Britain. The Romans may have left many legacies and influences behind them, but not when it came to the foundations of our legal system.

The Dark Ages is perhaps one of those periods in history that has, for many of us, quite literally stayed in the dark. Due to the fact that so little was documented in the 600 years following the Romans' departure, the name was given to this period in history by early historians to reflect this.

Now, however, we do know that the

second invaders of our island did have a big impact on our country and its laws. From around 400 A.D. foreign invasions were a frequent occurrence, particularly from Northern Germany and Southern Denmark – the Jutes, the Saxons, the Angles. It didn't take long for this variety of nationalities to be all lumped together under one name, the Saxons. Although Saxons had been landing on our shores during the Roman times, it wasn't until the Romans had departed that serious numbers of them were determined to make our country their home, with wives and children in tow.

Large parts of eastern England were taken over and controlled by the Saxons quite quickly, and with their extended families also having arrived, they soon formed many rural settlements. It is not known exactly how legal matters were settled in these early days, but we do know that everything from stealing a goat to murder was probably left to the judgement of the head of the family. If two neighbouring families fell out, then it was perfectly normal for them to take the law into their own hands and sort things out by spilling blood. The rules were very simple, by law, if

Settlements of Angles, Saxons and Jute in Britain about 600

Celtic peoples
Angles
Saxons
Jutes

anyone hurt you, you were allowed to retaliate and hurt them back.

After three generations of blood feuding, which meant in reality the killing of many members of the same family including women and

ABOVE
Roman Britain.

RIGHT
First Page of
Aethelbert's Laws.

The blood feuding was, however, probably only put into practice for the most grave of legal disputes. For any other misdemeanour or crime, the head of the family acted as the local law enforcer. This Saxon way was evidently very effective as the practice lasted for hundreds of years. A new influence then arrived that cast an entirely new angle on law in Britain, and funnily enough, it also came from across the water.

By the middle of the 1st millennium A.D., England was a Saxon land. The small, rural Saxon settlements as they began soon started joining together to form small kingdoms, and each with an appointed king who was in charge of dictating the laws of his people. One of these Saxon kings came under the influence of a complete outsider, and the result had a massive effect on the direction British law took thereafter.

In the year 597 A.D. our new invader, Saint Augustine, landed on our shores. Instead of being armed with the usual sword, this man was armed with a cross. Soon after he landed in Kent, he converted the local ruler there, King Aethelbert, by persuading him to do what they did on the

children when families seriously fell out, it mercifully came to an end. It seems extraordinary to think that that was the way legally, disputes were settled during Saxon times.

Christian continent – write down the law. Aethelbert's law code was the very first ever written in English, but it wasn't merely a more up-to-date version of the Ten Commandments. It contained an enormous amount of detail about a particular area of the law that one would probably assume to be very modern – compensation!

To understand it now, obviously needs translating from Old English. In summary, the document was indeed based on the basics of the Ten Commandments, i.e. laws against thieving, killing and adultery were all included. The document goes further than this, however, and goes into a huge amount of detail about specific injuries that could be inflicted on another person and how, if that happened, the protagonist would be liable to pay the victim compensation. For example, if a man were to break another man's arm, he would be liable to pay compensation of six shillings in old money, approximately £600 today. Due to it being seen as having a detrimental effect on the next generation, if a man's genitals were deliberately injured the compensation tag would have been

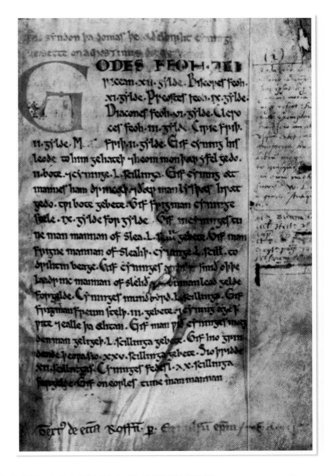

equivalent to around £60,000 now.

In today's society, value is still placed on body parts, although in modern law a similar injury to the last stated above is, in fact, only worth £30,000. Our modern compensation system is now a multi-billion pound industry with many thousands of claims made each year, and it is no stranger to controversy either. The hundreds of families and victims involved in the 7/7 London bombings were offered compensation by the British Government. How do you place a value on body parts and injury? It is a very difficult task, not to mention an extremely emotive one too.

In addition to having a compensation amount laid out for every limb, Aethelbert's law book also detailed the amount for loss of life and was based on a system called 'Weregild'. The word is made up of two, were – man, and gild – money, i.e. the money that you have to pay if you kill another man. Killing was a very expensive business in those days, especially if your target was say a king, whose price would have been around 12,000 shillings or c. £1.2 million. A nobleman would cost you 1,200 shillings or c. £120,000;

a peasant would have cost you 200 shillings or c. £20,000. Even an element of racism crops up in Anglo Saxon law: if you killed a Welshman it would only cost you 60 shillings or c. £6,000!

It wasn't long before Christianity had spread throughout the numerous Saxon kingdoms. This was the first time in our history the same law was codified the length and the breadth of the land. Each Saxon king had his own set of written down laws, known as 'domes'. By the end of the 10th century the Christian tradition of writing down laws had spread throughout the entire country.

Along with the arrival of Christianity came another idea – a powerful one – hell. This now meant that the fear of damnation was also in the minds of those being judged, so the morale pressure to tell the truth increased dramatically.

With that concept also came a development that is still very much with us today – the swearing of the religious oath.

As a witness or defendant in a court of law in the 21st century, the court requires you to swear that you will 'tell the truth, the whole truth and

nothing but the truth', and on the holy book of your religion if you are religious. In Saxon times, however, the religious oath was much more than just a promise to tell the truth, it was

the way the majority of legal disputes were resolved. It would have been a public event held in what were called 'hundred courts', of which there were many scattered in prominent places throughout the land. Simply swearing the religious oath was enough to settle most simple cases, because of the fear of eternal damnation. Sadly, this is not the case any more, and many (even high profile) people are sentenced today for lying under oath in court.

In Saxon England, if a dispute couldn't be settled by the swearing of oaths alone, then there was a second level – the church. Replacing the role that the heads of the villages had, priests were used to call on the judgement of God. Known as the 'trial by ordeal', the verdict would be decided by the outcome of a trial that the defendant would have to face. There would have been a choice of three, and all pretty gruesome: the trial by hot iron, which meant the accused would have to walk five paces carrying a lump of red hot metal; the second was the trial by cold water, which meant that the accused was thrown into a river and if they floated they were deemed guilty and if they sank deemed not guilty; the third was the trial by boiling water, and judgement was decided three days after the accused's hand had been bandaged up, following which they removed the dressing and if the hand had healed an innocent verdict would be passed, but if it was pussy and foul then the verdict would be guilty. This final method was also used to determine the guilt following the trial by hot iron.

Almost any crime could result in a trial by ordeal, from theft to sexual misconduct, right through to heresy and witchcraft. According to ancient manuscripts, there was a particular way that the trial had to be conducted. The doors of the church would be closed, just like they would be in a courtroom now, before the trial commenced.

If the accused failed a trial by ordeal the village elder still made the decision with regard to the punishment that would be inflicted. This ranged from a fine to the death penalty, and execution by hanging was the Saxon's preferred method.

The landscape itself was an important part of how Saxons were reminded about the power of the law

on a daily basis. The judicial meeting places or 'hundred courts' would have been on high points of the land that could have been visible for many miles. Combined with the church, where the actual trials took place, the guilty would be taken to the very boundary of the local community – the boundary of the hundred – where the hanging or decapitation would take place. The hanging gallows with bodies swinging from it would have been visible from a great distance.

The Dark Ages in Britain saw many important changes occur with the law, developing from the head of the family resolving disputes to judgement being in the hands of the local kings and God almighty. Even after death Saxon law continued and the way people were buried was highly ritualised; some were buried face down with their hands tied. This was to reassure the people living near the burial sites that even if the criminal came back to life in the grave, they could not possible dig out, they could only dig down; a fear of the dead coming back to haunt the living was a common concern.

Laws at this time were, however, still local, with the country divided into a number of kingdoms. The developments that resulted in the country being finally united under one king with a single set of laws came with the arrival of a new wave of people.

Around 780 A.D. the Vikings arrived, and in enormous numbers. Although their fearsome reputation precedes them, they were in fact quite a civilised bunch, many of them being farmers, settlers, and traders. They began by establishing their settlements all the way down the east coast of England, the area which became known as the 'Danelaw'. Danelaw stretched from Chester all the way down to London as the Vikings absorbed the Saxon kingdoms as they went. Saxon England was in danger of disappearing altogether, yet one kingdom held out, Wessex, whose leader would become a historical legend – Alfred the Great.

Alfred's dream was to create a united country and in his drive to achieve it, he would also transform our legal system. He first encountered the Vikings on the battlefield, but he was defeated and forced into hiding and had to travel in disguise. The famous story of Alfred burning a lady's cakes when he was in hiding at her house and too preoccupied with beating the Vikings is well known. Whether true or not, shortly after this supposed incident, Alfred rallied his troops and managed to defeat the Vikings. Although he never defeated them completely, he did manage to hold them at bay by making a truce with them. Then, clever Alfred harnessed the law as a weapon to sure up his kingdom of Wessex against the Vikings. One of

FAR LEFT
Alfred The Great.

LEFT
Location of
Wessex.

his first acts was to produce a written law code that compared him to Moses. The implication was that Alfred's laws were handed down from the very highest authority, and the English, therefore, were God's chosen people.

Some of Alfred's ideas were in fact very modern. For example, in his law codes he detailed how he thought people should be judged equally in the eyes of the law. By creating laws such as this, Alfred was determined

WHAT A BLOODY FEUD!

that by making Wessex a fair place to live it 'would make it more attractive compared with neighbouring Danelaw. It was Alfred's obsession with defeating the Vikings that drove him to being the great lawmaker that he became. Having halted their advance, he was hell bent on creating a kingdom that

had a powerful sense of Englishness, using ideology as a weapon of war.

The way the law was enforced was Alfred's next task. Just as today we have a legal hierarchy that culminates in the European Court of Justice, Alfred organised his courts so that there was an appeal system that could go all the way to the top, starting with the parish or 'hundred court'. From there one could appeal to the Shire Court, similar to our County Courts today, and then one could go to the highest court in the land, the King's Court, that of Alfred. Local people seemed to be entirely uninhibited about approaching him with legal problems.

Within 20 years of Alfred coming to power any Saxon areas that hadn't been overrun by the Vikings were firmly part of his Kingdom of Wessex. Alfred again used the law to consolidate that power and was well on his way to creating a united kingdom in England. In order to achieve his ultimate goal, however, Alfred needed the absolute loyalty of his people. Any boy or man over the age of 12 was required to swear an oath announcing their loyalty to the King; it was an extremely powerful way of ensuring that everyone knew who was in charge.

In modern society we don't have to declare our allegiance to the monarch, but since 2004 any immigrants applying for British citizenship have to take a test of which 75 percent has to be correctly answered to pass. Having passed that,

a special ceremony has to be attended during which all prospective British citizens have to swear allegiance to the Queen and promise to respect the United Kingdom's rights and freedoms.

For Alfred, the swearing of allegiance was very much a part of his ideological armoury in his struggle against the Vikings. He also made sure that all of his documents containing the law were written in plain, simple English. The literacy rate during Saxon times was poor, but it did mean that the law could be read out so that everyone

LEFT
Viking Expansion.

BELOW
Head of UK
Immigration.

understood it. It is perhaps a shame that we do not adhere to such simple, easy-to-understand methods today!

Bordering on obsessive, Alfred's interest in the law meant that he would study in enormous detail all of the decisions made by his judges. If he thought that they had made the wrong judgements or were not on top of his laws, he would challenge them directly and demand that they study the law properly before continuing in their duties. This is the first mention in English of anyone actually actively studying law – an enormous step forward with regard to our legal history.

Alfred was evidently an incredibly enlightened thinker, who also turned his attention to some outdated legal practices. Blood feuds were still an acceptable way of resolving serious disputes. Instead of being able to retaliate immediately following a crime for example, Alfred changed the law so that one had to wait seven days before any revenge could be taken. The original 'cooling off' period, it was an ingenious way of taking the heat out of the situation and allowing time for rational thought and consideration to happen.

Alfred died in 899 A.D. and although the Vikings were still around, due to his wise law reforms and the powerful sense of Englishness that he had instilled in his people, he had succeeded in sowing the seed for a country to be united under one monarch. The dream that he never lived to see came true 25 years after his death, when his grandson became the very first King of the whole of England.

By the end of the 1st millennium, Saxon England was a united a country with an accompanying and sophisticated set of laws. Although Alfred had put the laws in place, there were still many people who broke them. With no national police force as we know today, the law was enforced by the entire community being mobilised, using a legal device known as the 'hue and cry'. If someone saw a crime being committed, one was obliged by law to raise the 'hue and cry'. Everyone over the age of 15 who heard it was also legally obliged to form a group who would try and catch the criminal. If they were successful the criminal was put in front of the local law official, the sheriff, as they became known.

The office of sheriff is, in fact, still with us and not just consigned to the history books and westerns! We still have High Sheriffs in office who do things like reward local citizens for hard work, dedication to causes, helping the community etc. The ceremonies to award such people, however, are remarkably similar to the Saxon ones, with the Sheriff congratulating the man who responded to the 'hue and cry'. In King Alfred's day the sheriff was also a formidable and feared law enforcer with unrivalled local powers.

If a criminal managed to slip the 'hue and cry' he would become 'outside the law' or an 'outlaw'. Not quite as glamorous as the Robin Hood scenario would lead us to believe, being an outlaw in Saxon England would have been very grim. Being an outlaw meant that the law no longer controlled you, but it also meant that it no longer protected you either. Any land or property you owned would be given to the King and you'd be forced to live in hiding. If other law-abiding citizens discovered an outlaw, they were allowed to do whatever they liked with him. Of course, outlaws were also viewed as social outcasts. If an outlaw

LEFT Queen Elizabeth II.

repented, however, it was possible for them to be allowed back into society. If declared innocent following a second trial they would be named as 'a new person'. Any land or property handed over to the King prior to this would not, however, be returned.

The Anglo-Saxon period in history created a united country, with a fair set of laws and a sense of Englishness that is still with us today. They created a sophisticated system of courts and appeals, and they had legal professionals such as sheriffs. There is one final and crucial part to the story so far that is also believed to have started during this period – that of the jury. The very first story, be it true or not, consisted of 12 men judging a statue of the Virgin Mary that had apparently fallen of its own accord killing a local woman praying in church. Although the jury didn't become an established part of our legal system for another 200 years, this could have been the very first instance of trial by jury during the Saxon times. It seems that with regard to the law, the Dark Ages were certainly not as dark as they had first appeared to historians.

Knowledge is Power

9 00 years ago the entire business of establishing guilt and innocence was very different compared with the courtroom scenario that we know today, with judge, jury, and barristers.

Before 1066, justice was often random and brutal, and the law was often used as a tool to control the masses by instilling fear in them. The most important figure in law wasn't even human. In Medieval times, no man was allowed to pass judgement on another man; that was up to God. Trial, often held in churches, was where God's judgement would be revealed. The way of doing this (trial by ordeal) has already been discussed.

The trial with the hot metal rod, for example, was decided by whether the injury to the hand healed quickly or not. If it did, then the accused was innocent, if it took a long time or blistered or festered, it would have been a guilty verdict. It was mostly petty criminals or innocent peasants who endured this type of justice system. In

1066, however, when the Normans invaded, the entire population would begin to feel the full brutality of the law.

William the Conqueror and his army virtually wiped out the Saxon aristocracy and put the country under occupation. In addition to the strength of their military, they also knew how to use law to exert control over a rebellious population. The Normans

LEFT
Robin Hood.
BELOW
Trial by Battle.

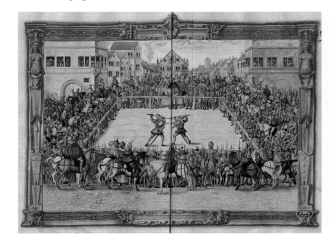

were also God-fearing people but they had some even more gruesome and gory ways of achieving divine justice.

Initially William approached King Harold II with the proposal that they could settle the argument about who was going to rule the country by having a one-on-one, man-to-man fight. This was after all the normal way that Norman men settled their disputes and was called 'trial by battle'. Harold refused, however, and the rest, as they say, is history! The two armies famously fought at the Battle of Hastings in 1066. Harold was killed and the Norman conquest of England began.

'Trial by battle' became part of English law and sat alongside 'trial by ordeal'. If a man was accused of a serious crime such as murder or rape, he could prove his innocence by fighting his accuser. These fights took place in front of a large crowd and would have had the atmosphere of a country fair nowadays! The fights came to an end only when one party either surrendered or was killed. This was still considered divine justice; the belief was that God would always ensure that the innocent man won. This method

also had some obvious pitfalls: relying on brute strength, it provided a legally sanctioned arena in which a big man could legally beat up a smaller enemy. Justice was indeed very brutal and if God's will said you were guilty, you could expect to be killed, mutilated, or at the very least severely humiliated.

We may imagine that 21st-century justice has come a very long way since this Norman brutality, although it may come as a surprise to find that some of these traditions may be making a comeback!

The 7,000 Norman invaders had the problem of controlling a population of around two million. Although they crushed opposition with sheer force, they also relied on the people within the communities to enforce the law.

After a criminal was locked up and maybe castrated and blinded (which was William the Conqueror's favourite punishment incidentally) the guilty would be led through the streets being whipped all the time before being placed in the pillory (similar to stocks) in the town's square. The jeering crowd would then be at liberty to throw anything at the criminal including stones

and excrement. It was not uncommon for people to die whilst in the pillory.

Public humiliation was a common punishment in Norman times and the best they could do to deter petty criminals without the presence of a police force. Even though the Normans ruled the entire country, justice was pretty haphazard to say the least and it all depended on where you lived; a kind of Norman time postcode lottery one might say. In Winchester, a convicted thief would be mutilated, in Dover he'd be thrown off a cliff, in Sandwich, he'd be buried alive, and in some seaport towns he'd be tied to a stake below the high water mark and left to drown. The punishment on a convicted criminal was a very local rather than national affair.

In 2006 in Bridlington in the East Riding of Yorkshire, the notion of local justice was reintroduced and the concept had something surprisingly in common with the Norman times – it involved public humiliation. Nine hundred years after the Norman invasion, Bridlington Council came up with a modern version of putting criminals in the stocks. They decided that ASBOs (Anti-Social Behaviour Orders) on their own weren't enough, so they instigated their own initiative that became known as the 'pillar of shame'. There were posters of all the local kids with ASBOs in the area stuck on a large round noticeboard in the centre of the town for everyone to see. As well as 'naming and shaming' the offenders, it also showed the local community who these people were so that the police could

be notified if they broke the conditions of the order. The human rights group Liberty thinks that the entire concept of 'naming and shaming' people is a dangerous route to go down, as well as being a massive step backwards.

Community justice may be controversial in the 21st century, but in Norman times it was the standard way of dealing with petty criminals. For an army trying to suppress an entire population, it was, however, never going to be enough. The Normans were very unpopular and were therefore being murdered by resistance fighters; local villages were concealing these killings. It got to the point when the Normans needed to do something about it once and for all, and they used the law to that effect.

For the first time in England's history its rulers were strong enough to enforce their justice system on the entire country. A law was therefore created that stated if any Norman was murdered and the culprit was handed over, then the entire village would be subject to a crippling fine. The law was named after the Latin for 'secret killing' – 'the murdrum fine'.

LEFT Jury Box.

The consequences of this new law were, however, rather unexpected. Villagers began dumping bodies of murdered Normans in other villages so that they got the blame and the fine. It was rife, with Norman bodies being moved and dumped all over the place!

Although not entirely foolproof, the new 'murdrum' law did symbolise a major shift in the law from the local stocks to justice on a national level. The Normans then took a further step forward with regard to nationalising the law with the first ever example of using state intelligence put into practice.

William the Conqueror was the first ruler of England who gathered information on his subjects. An enormous survey of the whole of England was carried out only 20 years after the Norman Conquest. The people labelled this the 'Domesday Book' due to the fact that it reminded them of judgement day. The 1086 Domesday survey was remarkably thorough and over only two years recorded details of over 13,000 settlements. With taxation in mind, the shrewd William used the information to ensure that he could collect the maximum taxes

possible from the English population. Those refusing to cooperate would have been severely punished.

Naturally, the English were deeply suspicious of all of the questions being asked of them. Of course they were right to be so, as what William was carrying out was a calculated exercise in state control. If he knew exactly who owned what and how much, then he could use that as a weapon against his people by threatening to take it away from them. Having completed his survey, William proceeded to call a meeting with all the landowners in the country and made them swear allegiance to him; unsurprisingly, not a soul refused.

The Normans had got to grips with the concept that knowledge was power, and had made the ideological step in realising that exerting control on a national rather than a local level was the way forward.

Surveillance is an integral part of our modern society, albeit sometimes controversially. There are some four million CCTV cameras throughout the United Kingdom, more than any other country in Europe. The Norman desire for information gathering has now become a modern-day obsession. All of our personal information is accessible to the state if they should so wish to look, including emails, tax and medical records, travel details, bank statements, mobile phone calls; the list is endless. The biometric passports and concept for ID cards will probably lead to a comprehensive national DNA database in the future. We are told that it is for our own safety, but many are deeply

concerned and are once again worried by this threat posed by the state 1,000 years after the Domesday survey.

Using the law to great effect, England was ruled with an iron fist during the reign of William the Conqueror. The Domesday Book and 'murdrum fine' were impressive measures that helped the Normans maintain control over their subjects on a national scale. This, however, was not to last.

KNOWLEDGE IS POWER

Following the death of William in 1989, the Norman dynasty began to fall apart. This led to 20 years of national chaos and civil war. The country started splitting up once again as powerful barons seized control of different areas, at the same time reverting back to taking the law into their own hands. The brutal Norman regime may have gone, but this was replaced by arguably an even worse state of affairs, that of injustice and therefore misery. The country's fortunes only began to change in 1154, when William's great grandson Henry II claimed the English throne.

Now, a century after the first Normans arrived on our shores, the enlightened new King turned the old Norman laws on their head and in doing so began a revolution with regard to justice.

Judges as we know them today (apart from wearing funny wigs and red robes) are very much part of the legal establishment and they sit in judgement on anyone who breaks the law, from ordinary citizens to politicians and even the royal family. They didn't have so much clout back in the 12th century, however, and their rise to power happened almost by chance.

With the country and legal system in tatters by the time Henry II took the throne, he urgently needed to build respect for the law and reassert authority over the people of England. To achieve this he chose less brutal and more sophisticated methods. Pulling together a team of senior judges, he sent them all over the country. These travelling justices had the power to overrule the local sheriffs with the specific task of ensuring that the law of the King was implemented throughout the entire country. They were so successful in fact that Henry's judges are still with us 800 years later.

We still have modern day travelling or touring judges, known as 'red' judges or High Court Judges. They travel around the country taking their expertise with them, judging over some of the country's most difficult cases. There is also still very much tradition and ceremony with what goes on today, a great deal of which the judges of the 12th century would have recognised. In fact, the job of our modern touring judges is very similar to that of Henry II's inasmuch as their job is to make sure that justice is carried out in the same way throughout the country. Although, of course, Henry II had additional motives: keeping the barons in order as well as raising taxes.

Henry II's judges were a vital part of his strategy by spreading the tentacles of royal authority all around the country. Inadvertently, however, he also unleashed a formidable legal force, a force that would eventually be in a position to sit in judgement over the King himself. Charles I became a victim of these legal powers 450 years after Henry II, when he was tried and executed for treason.

A secondary benefit was also initiated when Henry sent his judges around the country, which would lead to one of the most important and unique aspects of our legal system.

The judges travelled around with royal authority along with a lot of pomp and ceremony. There were still countless different laws and procedures throughout the country, which forced them to use their own expertise and discretion when passing judgement. Returning to London they would have compared the judgements they had made with other fellow judges,

but with the number of judgements being made it turned into a logistical nightmare. How could any new judge be expected to take in this ridiculous amount of information?

Henry's most senior judge, Glanville, came up with, what turned out to be, a fantastic idea. He decided to write all of the judgements down in one book. This meant that all the judgements could be circulated and then applied throughout the country in a consistent way, therefore initiating the process of standardising the law. The result of which was what came to be known as 'English Common Law'.

Glanville's first book was a small guide for judges with all the new and existing laws contained in it, and it was called *The Treaties on the Laws and Customs of the Kingdom of England*. Glanville had started something revolutionary without even knowing it. From then on every law that was made and every judgement that was passed had to be written down. So much written law now exists that it is thought it would take a person 450 years to read it all in its entirety!

The significance of this 'Common

Law' has had an enormous impact on us today. It has become the foundation for all legal systems in civilised and even some parts of uncivilised societies throughout the world. It has left us a heritage of legal aspects such as jury trial, professional lawyers, judiciary, and people who will stand up to the government when they have to.

Henry II therefore put in place two pillars of our existing legal establishment – independent judges and the foundation of English Common Law. This also implies, however, that everything under Henry's reign was fair and equal. Although Henry's judges were responsible for overseeing trials and announcing punishments, the guilty or innocent verdict was still at this time left to God.

Divine judgement had reigned supreme for centuries; both Norman systems of 'trial by battle' and 'trial by ordeal' were still the primary legal procedures of establishing guilt or innocence. By the time of Henry II, however, church leaders were beginning to question the practice of subjecting the accused to such ordeals. This was not because they thought it barbaric

or unjust, but they simply thought it was wrong to expect God to be at their beck and call at the drop of a hat to make such decisions! Finally in the year 1215, Pope Innocent III banned both ordeal practices once and for all.

For the very first time in criminal trials, justice decided by a person and not God was about to enter the courts of law. Although God was no longer called upon during a trial, they did still take place in his house, and in the year 1220 a legal revolution was instigated by accident and involved a woman called Alice.

Finding herself in trouble with the law, Alice accused five men of theft in an attempt to save her own skin. With no 'trials' allowed, they had to work out a way of proving the guilt or innocence of these men. In the days of the 'trial' system, the accused had on occasion been allowed to bring up to 12 family and friends to give evidence under oath; they were know as juries. With no other legal means to reach a verdict for Alice's case, the court decided, for the very first time, to summon a jury to actually settle the case. The jury were also for the first time going to be

LEFT
Pope Innocent III.

picked at random by the court in order to avoid any bias that would inevitably come from using people chosen by the accused. Although the men agreed to this, they soon wished they hadn't – the jury found one of them innocent, but pronounced the other four as thieves and they were promptly hanged. By saving her own skin, Alice initiated a system that has been with us ever since: trial by jury had arrived.

The new jury system didn't, however, take off immediately. The old trial systems by ordeal based on God's divine judgement couldn't be argued with, but the decisions of fallible men could.

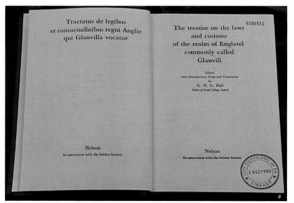

It was therefore decided that a trial by jury should be a voluntary choice made by the accused and judges certainly didn't always find it easy persuading them to accept a trial by jury. Even though the court picked the jury, they would almost certainly have been neighbours of the accused; this also meant that the jurors could be as biased against them as they could for them.

With many possible criminals going unpunished because of this, it was not long before the judges decided to put their collective foot down. Their resolution was to inflict a little gentle persuasion on the accused, in the form of weights. The bottom line was, that if you kept refusing a trial by jury, you would end up being crushed to death! Ironically, many preferred the option of being crushed to death, rather than being found guilty by a jury and then inevitably hung. By avoiding a hanging all of your worldly possessions would be left to your family, rather than the Crown taking everything.

Regardless of the fact that the jury system has been around for eight centuries, it still often comes under attack, with the cost of it often the reason nowadays or the fact that the jury do not understand the details of a complicated case. It could be argued that we'd be better off just letting the legal professionals make the decisions and get rid of juries altogether. This, however, fills many with fear, as it would lead to just one class of people receiving the justice and another class of people receiving it. This could ultimately lead to a lack of legitimacy and trust within the legal system. The argument for keeping juries lies in the fact that they have common sense, life experience, come from all different walks of life and they really are the best people to decide if someone is telling the truth or not.

So, three major pillars of our legal system had been put in place 150 years after the Norman invasion – independent judges, trial by jury, and the Common Law. They had, nonetheless, all evolved with the sole aim of allowing the King to keep his power; they therefore also required his support. With the departure of Henry II and his son King John on the throne, things began to change and he used his power ruthlessly and even tried to turn the legal clock back; unlike his

father, King John had very little respect for justice. When King John's barons refused to contribute to his war chest, he increased taxes, stole their land and locked them up without trial. This, unsurprisingly, sparked off a rebellion and the free barons took control of London and Lincoln that brought the entire country to the verge of civil war.

Just in time, however, something extraordinary happened in a field in Surrey that put the King well and truly back in his place. After all the unrest caused by the King's behaviour, the barons finally got him to back down and agree to their demands. A simple document called the 'Magna Carta' changed the world forever. The barons prepared the document that limited the King's powers and forced him to accept the idea that everyone in the country should have rights under the law. The two sides met at the meadows in Runnymede in Egham, Surrey to do the deal and exchange the 'kiss of peace'.

Naturally and rightly so, the barons were still suspicious of King John and they insisted that copies of the signed Magna Carta were circulated throughout the entire kingdom. This is why the Magna Carta survived and became one of the most famous legal documents in the whole world.

The Magna Carta contains some 63 clauses, most of them righting fairly minor wrongs. One or two clauses have, however, become fundamental cornerstones of our legal system: no one could be detained without charge or sufficient evidence (also known as 'habeas corpus'), and everyone had the right to a fair trial. Habeas corpus is a key element in the concept of English justice because it dictates that you can't hold a person without a trial for more than a relatively short period of time; now 24 hours in the United Kingdom. Even in recent times when this basic right has been violated, the resulting fallout has been significant. The unrest in Northern Ireland in the 1970s is a good example of this.

Although habeas corpus is enshrined within our law, it appears to be less significant when our country is seriously under threat. In 2004, eight terror suspects were held in Belmarsh Prison and they were never charged or put on trial, but were being held indefinitely. They were eventually

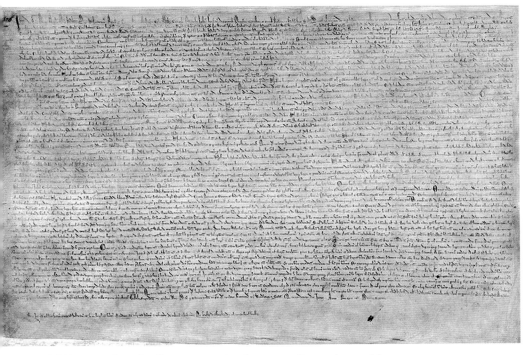

released following a lengthy dispute between the independent judges in the House of Lords and the government.

The birth and circulation of the Magna Carta all those years ago not only eventually influenced legal systems all over the world, but it instilled fundamental human rights into our legal practices. At the time of King John, however, this didn't necessarily mean that fair justice reigned in England.

Freedom of Speech

Freedom of speech is an aspect of our everyday lives and law that some of us probably take for granted. Arriving at this liberal state did not happen overnight, however, it was a hard won right that goes back to the time of the Tudor King Henry VIII.

Henry VIII came to the throne in 1509 and the country he took over already had a pretty well established legal system. As an absolute monarch, like nearly every king that went before him, if Henry VIII wanted something then it got done. Parliament was little more than a technical rubber stamp for the King's wishes. This meant that the only person who was really allowed to say whatever he wanted was the King himself.

In 16th-century England if an ordinary person spoke their mind they could get into serious trouble. Within Henry's parliament, however, there was one man who thought that it was time changes were made; his name, Thomas Moore.

A brilliant politician and a truly courageous man, Thomas Moore was a radical thinker who proposed a change in the law that would directly challenge the absolute power of the King. In 1523 even though Moore was Speaker of the House of Commons, it wasn't a God-given right that even someone of his standing could say what he liked; one could get into serious trouble by saying the wrong thing. Speaking out against the King's laws and ending up in the Tower of London was not at all uncommon. Thomas Moore therefore displayed extreme audacity when, directed at the King, he requested freedom of speech for members of parliament. This was the first time in English history that anyone had ever argued the case for freedom of speech in parliament. It was Thomas Moore who set the ball rolling that resulted in the freedom of speech laws we have today.

A man ahead of his time, perhaps, Moore's proposal was undoubtedly regarded as just about as radical as it came in the 16th century. Even today though, things do not always run smoothly and the law is an ever changing and often controversial subject. For example, in 2005 the government passed a law that banned the right to demonstrate in Parliament Square, claiming that it

was for reasons of national security; some, however, regarded it as an erosion of the rights to protest, and that the advancement of freedom of speech rights have in fact regressed

by about 40 years in recent times.

The court of Henry VIII did not take kindly to Moore's suggestion, and it was another 150 years before members of parliament were granted that right. But what Moore did do was plant the seed of the idea in people's minds. Henry VIII therefore remained very much in control for the time being.

With Henry doing as he pleased, his next major step ended up in tearing Europe in half. Due to the fact that the law is ultimately all about power, those who make the laws inevitably use them to increase the power they can exert over others. The 16th century saw the beginning of one of the country's biggest ever power struggles in the history of England, and one that would take 150 years to be resolved for good.

In 1527 Henry started one enormous row with the only existing major rival to his authority – the Roman Catholic Church. Bearing in mind that the church owned approximately one-tenth of properties in the country and could also raise its own taxes, it was therefore a very wealthy establishment. It also had great legal powers with its own law courts, and ultimately this was not controlled in England, but by the Pope in Rome.

Clement VII was the Pope at the time and it was his take on the laws of marriage that gave the King such a problem. In order to divorce his first wife even Henry VIII needed special permission granted from Rome. When the Pope refused Henry's request, he took the law into his own hands and set up his own church – the Church of England. Naturally, he made himself the head of it. He then introduced the Act of Supremacy, which were a set of laws that would have a massive impact on the future direction of the country.

What this actually meant was that he had separated Britain from the influences of Rome and launched it instead on a path of independence from the rest of Europe. This legislation therefore made Henry the head of the state and head of the church, making him more powerful than any monarch before, or in fact since. The extra powers that the Act of Supremacy gave him, amongst other things, meant that he could now tell other people what their religion was, and if they didn't agree they could be charged as traitors and sentenced to death.

The split from Rome affected every level of society. The fact that he was now in charge of the church had implications for every man, woman and child in the country. With the Catholic monasteries and monks destroyed and run out of town, anything that would once have been paid to the monks was now automatically paid to Henry VIII; he was to all intents and purposes now a dictator.

Keeping the country Anglican and out of the hands of the Catholic Church was, however, his main priority. Having a son and heir to take over from him was therefore of paramount importance. His first wife Catherine of Aragon only had girls, his second wife Anne Boleyn only had girls, Jane Seymour, his third, did produce a son, Edward, who became King, but he died when he was only 15 years old. Henry's other three wives didn't produce any children at all. So, who was going to be heir? The answer was Edward's half-sister Mary, but she was a staunch Catholic and became known throughout history as Bloody Mary.

Queen Mary I did everything in

her power to hand control of the church back to Rome by ripping up her father's laws and spending the five years of her reign burning 363 Protestants for heresy; more than any had been burnt in the previous 200 years. Queen Elizabeth I succeeded her half-sister when she died in 1558 and the atmosphere changed instantly. Elizabeth was Protestant, and although she reinstated the Church of England, she chose not to use the power of the law to persecute people of different faiths. She instead performed a delicate balancing act trying to appease people of all faiths. Elizabeth wanted to show the world that she was a much better ruler than her sister Mary had been.

Today, 400 years after the age of the Tudors, most people would agree that religious freedom is absolutely necessary in a modern democracy. Even though the right to freely practise your religion of choice is guaranteed in this country, we are still struggling to find the most suitable way for the law to deal with religion; making the law fair for everyone is certainly a tricky business. Although religious tolerance means accepting other people's belief

systems, the effect can be extremely dangerous when they begin to actually start threatening the established social order and even people's lives.

Something very similar in fact happened in 16th-century England. Having done everything she could to keep all religions happy as Elizabeth had done, a law issued on the Continent was about to destroy all her good work. The new Pope in Rome, Pius V, viewed Elizabeth as a wicked infidel and his intention was to do everything in his power to bring Britain back under his Catholic control. In 1570 he issued a Papal bull. This was an order from the Pope to Catholics throughout the world stating that Queen Elizabeth was a heretic, and it was the duty of all Catholics to try and get rid of her.

This move forced Elizabeth to abandon her once tolerant view of religion and she turned her attention to getting rid of any fanatical Catholics or Jesuits who threatened her life. With the circulation of the Papal bull she also went about adjusting laws to help her cause. Those laws that were once not too serious, such as paying a shilling fine if you didn't attend church regularly,

LEFT Mary II.

turned into much more serious offences with more serious consequences for those who disobeyed by showing allegiance to the Pope. Officially it was alright to be a Catholic because the Queen did not persecute people for their faith, but in reality, a practising Catholic would have been rebranded as a traitor under the political banner, not the religious one. The consequences meant being fined, jailed or killed, so it was in fact still persecution, albeit under a different guise.

This persecution continued into the reign of the next monarch, King James I. It was during this period that one group of Catholics, deciding enough was enough, put one of the most famous terrorist plots into place – the Gunpowder Plot. With the intention of striking at the very heart of the British establishment to put an end to their problems, in 1605 Robert Catesby rallied 10 other men, including Guy Fawkes. It was a remarkably simple plan: to blow up King James at the State Opening of Parliament on 5th November. In preparation for the attack, Catesby, Fawkes and the other conspirators managed to stash

36 barrels of gunpowder into a cellar room, close enough it is thought, to blow up parliament three times over. As most people are well aware, their cunning plan failed as a result of betrayal, and again, the rest is history. Guy Fawkes was caught red handed and alongside his co-conspirators was tortured and executed. The country, however, was in shock at just how close these religious extremists had got to pulling off the biggest terrorist attack the country would have ever seen.

Little needs to be said about how similar fears are very much with us today with regard to religious fanaticism and the damage, destruction and death that can ensue from it if successful.

Following the 7/7 London bombings the security forces were naturally in a state of high alert. This led to certain sections of society suddenly finding themselves under suspicion. The fallout of this emergency that caused widespread national panic meant that for some the consequences were extreme. Two weeks after the bombings the panic climaxed and a Brazilian electrician was shot and killed by armed police at Stockwell underground station in London. They mistook Jean Charles de Menezes for someone else they suspected of terrorist activity, yet others accused the police of overreaction and panic. It is doubtful that the order to 'shoot and kill' would have been given if it hadn't been for the heightened state of alarm the country was in at the time.

In modern society the balance between protecting people and giving them their freedom is the aim. In reality, however, this is not so easy and the balance constantly moves like a pendulum between the two as events change or occur. The laws that were passed after the 7/7 bombings and 9/11 terrorist attacks categorically changed things and many new laws were passed as a result. It remains to be seen if this was just a temporary adjustment of the legal pendulum or the start of something much more sinister.

Similarly, following the failed Gunpowder Plot more new laws were passed that actively discriminated against Catholics. They were no longer allowed to become lawyers or officers in the armed forces, and they had their right to vote taken away. Catholics would have to wait a further 200 years

LEFT Guy Fawkes.

before they got that back again. The tradition of Bonfire Night began in 1606, and the anti-Catholic feeling was so strong at the time that it was not a figure of Guy Fawkes that was burnt, as we recognise the tradition today, it was an effigy of the Pope.

Protestants were persecuted first, and then it was the Catholics' turn. The fact was that if your religious faith didn't fit in with the politics of the time, and more dangerously, newly constructed knee-jerk legislation, then the legal pendulum would swing away from protection towards control and oppression. For the Catholics, it swung in the opposite direction only 50 years later and the result was the execution of a King.

With regard to the history of our law, the following period proves to be a critical turning point. The absolute power of the monarch that had been built up by the Tudors was about to be overturned during the reign of the Stuarts. Henry VIII had put virtually all of the power of the law into his own hands, and his daughters also used that power to supress religious freedom. The entire balance of power began to

shift under the next monarch, King James I, with fundamental implications with regard to the development of the law. This turned out to be fatal in fact for his son Charles.

In the United Kingdom nowadays power is split three ways: the government, parliament, and the judiciary. They all have different functions and they are by and large equal in many ways. It was certainly not like that at the time of King James. The judiciary and parliament were much less significant with regard to actual power, the vast majority of which was still held in the hands of the King.

King James had a shock in store, however, as the monarchy was about to be confronted by the power of the judges. In 1607 another brave man decided that it was time to stand up to the authority wielded by the monarch. The catalyst was caused by the Archbishop of Canterbury complaining to the King about his judges, accusing them of meddling in affairs that shouldn't concern them, particularly with any matters relating to the church. He wanted jurisdiction over that and the King agreed with him.

LEFT James I.

Sir Edward Coke (now pronounced Cook), Chief Justice of all England made a speech to the King that was a pivotal moment in legal history, the result of which would end up transforming our law. The crux of the matter was down to the fact that the law, dished out by judges, should apply to everyone, including the King. This was an extremely radical notion in 1607. Unsurprisingly, the King did not agree. He believed in his divine right to be King and to be above the law. He had absolutely no intention of being subject to the power of the judges and that was the end of it. The concept that had been put to the King became known as the principle of the 'Golden Metwand'. King James's son, Charles I followed in his father's ideological footsteps, although with rather less success.

In 1642, King Charles I ordered the House of Commons to raise taxes so that a war could be fought against France. The MPs did not support him in the slightest, and war was declared instead between the King and Parliament. This resulted in the biggest contest for law-making power that this country has ever seen. Eventually, everyone was forced to take one side or the other, which inevitably led to a bloody civil war breaking out. The stakes were high; whoever won would have

LEFT
Oliver Cromwell.
BELOW Charles I.

total control of the future direction of the country and its laws.

The English Civil War raged for seven years, but eventually, under the command of generals such as Oliver Cromwell, the parliamentarians won the bloody battle. Parliament was now in control and in a totally unprecedented move, the King was put on trial for waging war on his people.

The trial began on the 20th January 1649 in the Great Hall at Westminster. In addition to MPs, soldiers and members of the public packing the Great Hall, also present were 68 judges. The King was charged with High Treason and other high crimes. Even in this situation, the King would not submit a plea of guilty or not guilty as he refused to acknowledge that the court had the power to try him in the first place. The King said the following: 'I would know by what power I am called hither, and when I know by what lawful authority, I shall answer'.

The case against the King took seven days to hear (a long trial in those days as most would only last a couple) and he still refused to enter a plea. Andrew Broughton, the Clerk of the Court, read out the verdict: 'The court does judge that the said Charles Stuart, as tyrant, traitor, murderer, and public enemy to the people of this good nation, shall be put to death by the severing of his head from his body'.

King Charles, having listened in silence to the verdict being read out, then protested and demanded the right to speak, but he was removed from the Great Hall to await his execution. It is said that the King wore two shirts on his execution day, so that he would not shiver and seem afraid in front of the crowd. He made a short speech, still proclaiming his divine right to be King, then laid his head on the block. After a couple of prayers the executioner took his head off with one blow of the axe.

The beheading of King Charles signalled the end of 800 years of an unbroken line of monarchs; the law was now totally under the jurisdiction of parliament for the first time in our country's history. The precedent had been set in stone with the principles of the Golden Metwand, i.e. that nobody is above the law and that the same rules shall be applied to absolutely everyone, regardless of their position in society.

Taking a member of the British royal family to court did not happen again until 350 years later. In November 2002, Princess Anne was subjected to a court trial after her dog attacked two children in Windsor, Surrey. It is a good example of how a member of the royal family was answerable to the same laws that we are. Princess Anne fortunately didn't lose her head over the matter; a fine of £1,000 sufficed!

Following the beheading of King Charles I, the country was facing an entirely new situation; it was without a monarch and ruler. Although the outcome of the Civil War had promised greater things for the country, it was not going to be a smooth ride.

Needing a leader, parliament turned to one of the great generals of the Civil War, Oliver Cromwell. The first thing that Cromwell's new government did was try and remove all trace of the old monarchy. One of the most controversial decisions he made was to keep the

LEFT
Oliver Cromwell.

FREEDOM OF SPEECH

theatres closed. At the time theatres were the principle form of entertainment for the mass of ordinary people. They had been shut during the Civil War to prevent public disorder, but were not reopened under Oliver Cromwell. Their main form of cultural entertainment had been stopped. The impact of this was equivalent to someone going round banning every household from watching television in today's society.

The theatre issue was just one of many parliamentarian changes that the new regime put in place. In 1649, after turning themselves into a Republic, they abolished the House of Lords. They then embarked upon some law reform: the sovereignty of parliament; the independence of the judiciary; the end of torture; and the freedom of worship and religion. These were not only enormous achievements in the history of our country, but in the world.

Unfortunately, Cromwell's initial good intentions of being a radical and enlightened law reformer didn't last forever. It was only a few years after he'd got rid of the King for tyranny that Cromwell himself used military force to dissolve parliament and he even started insisting on people addressing him as 'Your Highness'.

The 11 years that Cromwell was in charge was the only period in British history when our country was a Republic. Cromwell died in 1658 and by 1660 Britain reinstated the monarchy, with more bloody turmoil to come.

Charles II returned from France, and even though he threw out many of Cromwell's laws, many of the key protectorate principles that he had initiated were engrained in the conscience of the British people; their time would soon return.

At last, early under Charles II, the theatres were reopened. He also introduced one further legal custom that has been with us ever since. He spent his time in exile in France where wigs were all the rage as a way of covering up bald patches. This trend was led by King Henry III, followed by his loyal and fashion conscious courtiers. King Charles II loved the wigs and so brought the fashion statement back to England with him; as in France, soon everyone was wearing them, including judges.

Wig wearing is a custom that is still very much part of the legal profession. As a social fashion trend, however, it died out for everyone else in the 19th century.

With his preoccupation for theatres and wigs one has to wonder if Charles II made any fundamental changes during his reign. In fact he did, that being the independent jury. In a 17th-century courtroom jurors pretty much just did as they were told and it was the judge who really decided the verdict. That procedure was changed forever following one particular trial.

There was a case involving two Quakers, William Penn and William Meade, in 1667 who were arrested after preaching and charged with 'violent assembly'. The case went to trial by jury and the judge recommended to the jury to find them guilty. When the jury returned to the courtroom after deliberating the case, however, they proclaimed that they thought the men were innocent. The judge was so furious that the jury were locked up. The jury absolutely refused to give in and this led to the judge imposing a fine on them. Eventually a second judge was brought in who thought that the jury couldn't be punished by the first judge

just because he thought they had made an 'incorrect' decision, and the jury were released. In historical terms, this was the first instance where the principles of an independent jury were upheld.

Judges were, however, still intimidating figures, so although the theory of an independent jury had been born, in practice judges still managed to force the verdict of their choice on the jury. The show trials against Protestant rebels who threatened the reign of James II in 1685, historically known as the 'Bloody Assizes', is a powerful example of this. The armed rebels were heavily defeated in their quest to topple James II and a series of brutal trials ensued, which took place at a variety of locations across the West Country. These trials were not, however, about justice, they were about revenge.

Judge Jeffreys, known as the 'hanging judge' was in charge of the whole affair. Within five days some 300 rebels had been rushed through a cursory trial with the jury bullied into sending dozens of them to their death, by hanging. Jeffreys also sentenced those deemed of treason to the grotesque punishment of being 'drawn and quartered' as well.

Unsurprisingly, the nation was horrified at this abuse of royal and judicial power, and within three years James II had become so unpopular that he was driven out of the country by what became known as the 'Glorious Revolution'. First cousins William and Mary, who were imported from Holland, replaced him to become King William III and Queen Mary II. This time, however, with strict conditions. They had to agree to an Act of Parliament that massively restricted their legal authority – the Bill of Rights of 1688.

The importance of the Bill of Rights is on a level with the Magna Carta in terms of national significance. This set in stone all of the progress that had been made since the tyrannical days of Henry VIII. The 1688 Bill of Rights was historically monumental and over 200 years the law had been transformed. It allowed MPs freedom of speech in parliament; punishment had to be fair not cruel; monarchs were not allowed to raise taxes for their own personal gain; and the monarch could no longer send the country to war without the express permission of parliament.

LEFT James II.

Laws Grind the Poor, Rich Men Make the Law

As our politicians so often remind us, we are very privileged and fortunate to be living in a democracy. Unlike some other countries, we live in a society where our fundamental rights are protected by law. We have free elections, and the majority of us can vote for our personal choice of MP. Ultimately, this means that we all, to some degree, have a say in what laws are made by voting against a particular political party if we don't agree with what they stand for, or where they would like to take the country in the future. Back in the 18th century, that kind of democracy still had a long way to go.

From 1714 to 1830 the English throne was occupied by four King Georges. As we already know, by the Georgian period, the King did not have ultimate power of the country and its people; parliament was in charge of law making. On the surface this appears to be much more fair and equal. The fact was, however, that only three percent of the population were allowed to vote, meaning that only a very small minority of the British people were represented; a handful of wealthy men.

The aristocracy were responsible for electing parliament and as a result, often made laws to benefit themselves. This was certainly a golden age for both landed gentry and successful businessmen, all busy building their fortunes and empires. For these very privileged in society it was a great age of freedom. They were free to trade, to buy property, to make money, and they had a very nice life indeed. Strangely enough, the only reason they had such carte blanche in life was because it was these very men that made the laws in the first place.

As the saying goes 'an Englishman's home is his castle'. That was most certainly the mantra of the Georgian

LAWS GRIND THE POOR, RICH MEN MAKE THE LAW

general agreement that it was there to keep the common folk in order. As the Georgian maxim reflects: 'laws grind the poor, and rich men make the law'.

The enormous estates that the gentry accumulated were to be protected at any cost. For example, a judge called Edward Christian kept a gun under his bed for security and would have shot anyone who threatened his property, safe in the knowledge that the law would have been on his side.

The legality of taking pot shots at intruders is sadly, some would argue, not part of our life today. The famous case of the Norfolk farmer Tony Martin is an excellent example of the controversy this has caused in recent times. He was sentenced to a life in prison after he shot two intruders, killing one of them. This verdict caused a certain amount of public outrage, as many believed that he was the victim and should not have been punished. Today, 'reasonable force' is legally allowed if faced with this situation. In this particular case, Martin was accused of using unreasonable force in defending his property.

In the 18th century there was no such division, and whatever force

ruling classes. For these men, 'his home' included his property, wife, servants, dogs and furniture, and should be well protected at all times. It was a popular belief that the government was solely there to protect wealth and property. Making society a better place for the masses was surely not a job for the government? Although, there was deemed necessary was acceptable when protecting a wealthy man's castle. Parliament totally supported the concept and passed one of the most draconian laws against property crime our country has ever seen. In 1723, a gang of men were caught poaching in Waltham Forest. Normally poaching was an offence that attracted a fine, but nothing more, and in some circumstances was actually legal. Under traditional Forest Rights, poor people did have some rights to the natural produce growing or living in their landlord's forest. These men, however, had blackened faces. Having decided to tighten up on the Forest Rights' laws (mainly due to the fact that the landowners could make much more money by selling their produce) poaching with a blackened face was made a hanging offence. In addition to this, there were 49 other offences listed that were now also punishable by death and nearly all of them were to do with crimes against property. By the end of the century, the aristocracy had put in place almost 200 offences that carried the sentence of death, and some were for very petty crimes, pickpocketing for example.

These were extremely excessive measures and were an indication of just how insecure the ruling classes really felt. Even though they made the laws of the land, they evidently didn't feel safe without these additional draconian measures being added to the list. It was true that crimes such as muggings,

LAWS GRIND THE POOR, RICH MEN MAKE THE LAW

theft and highway robbery were all very common, particularly due to the fact that there was such a massive difference in wealth between the rich and the poor. Having been shot whilst travelling on his horse through Hyde Park in London, one MP wrote: 'one is forced to travel even at noon as if one is going into battle'! Of course there was still no police force, so the only deterrent that could be used to fight crime by the government was fear.

Now known as the Old Bailey or the Central Criminal Court, criminals caught for a capital crime, such as the poachers caught in Waltham Forest, would have been sent there. Known at the time as Newgate Prison, it was the home of the notorious 'hanging judges'.

In the 1700s everything was designed to instil fear in people. As well as the obvious fear of the gallows, the layout of courtrooms, for example, was designed to create maximum impact with regard to respect and awe of the law. The shackled defendant sat alone in the dock with the judge up high in front, and the jury up high to one side. It was like a theatre, with people paying to see the moment of high drama,

when the judge announced the verdict. Naturally, this was done in style too, with wig and red robe adorned and the black cap in hand, which was donned to pronounce the sentence of death.

Prisons as we know them today didn't exist in the 1700s. Criminals were only held in cells if they were either awaiting trial or awaiting the death penalty. Given only bread, water and gruel, three or four prisoners would have been crammed into a small rat-infested, typhoid-ridden cell.

Sending prisoners to their death was the only real way to deal with convicted criminals; nobody had come up with an alternative solution and there weren't any large prisons. Transportation was another solution, but this was reserved for those who had been pardoned from execution.

For those who had fallen foul of the King's law, execution it usually was, as a testament to the power of those in authority. On the day of execution a prisoner would have been given Holy Communion, shackled, and then led out of the cell to begin the journey to the gallows. The drama of the courtroom was in fact nothing compared to the

biggest spectacle of the time, a public hanging. It would have been extremely noisy, and in London particularly, a turnout of some 20,000 people would be witness to the day's gruesome events. Bearing in mind that many crimes went unpunished, a public hanging was a powerful tool for the state to remind its citizens of the possible consequences of such actions, as well as showing them that they were doing their job well.

When the whole procession arrived at the execution ground, it was usually in a field that had been turned into a theatre just days before the executions were due to take place. In London the traditional site was at Tyburn, a settlement west of the City. The hanging frame consisted of three uprights held together with three crosspieces. Each crosspiece could have up to eight ropes attached, therefore 24 people could have been hanged at the same time.

As the cart carrying the condemned

LAWS GRIND THE POOR, RICH MEN MAKE THE LAW

pulled up under the frame, the noose would be placed around the victim's neck and a sack placed over the face. The last words were then read by the chaplain: 'You have been adjudged by the laws of this country, unworthy any longer to live, unworthy to walk this earth, unworthy to breathe its air and that no further good to mankind can be expected from you, only the example of your death to warn others from the same ruin in the future. And may God have mercy on your soul'. Just before

the actual hanging the enormous crowd would have fallen silent as hats were taken off. If people needed reminding of the gruesome end that they could face if they fell foul of the law, then witnessing a public hanging would have been enough; it was an extremely powerful tool for the government.

Of course, with the change in laws and the additional 200 offences, hanging became a common event. It is thought that an average commoner living in London during the 1780s could have been witness to the deaths of about 1,200 people.

It is perhaps understandable that during this period crimes of the most serious nature, such as murder, were dealt with in this way. The problem was that even minor crimes, such as setting fire to a haystack, would be punishable by hanging as well. The authorities dished out death sentences as if they were giving away sweets; it was almost as if they were afraid of their own people.

The uncontrollable nature of a large group of commoners, also called a 'mob', was one of the aspects of society that the Georgian gentry were most afraid of. This anxiety didn't just come out of nowhere. Destruction and devastation had been caused by such events in the past. In a society where ordinary people were powerless to change the law, violent riots by large crowds were all too common, and could last for several days at a time.

Serious outbreaks of public disorder are still with us, albeit thankfully less frequently. The 1980s and 90s saw numerous protests turn into riots over the miners' strike and the poll tax, which threatened to destabilise Margaret Thatcher's government. As in the past, the response from the government was to introduce new laws, such as the Public Order Act of 1986. This new Act ultimately gave the police much more power to restrict public protest.

The most serious and society shaking to date were the England riots that took place between 6th and 10th August 2011 when several London boroughs and districts of cities and towns across England suffered widespread rioting, looting and arson. The riots were of such an unprecedented scale that the Prime Minister and other government leaders abandoned their summer holidays, all police leave was cancelled,

ABOVE
French Revolution, Storming of the Bastille.

and parliament was recalled on 11th August to debate the grave situation the country suddenly found itself in. With regard to the legal system, it was reported that some courts were advised by senior justice clerks to deal more harshly than usual with offences committed during the riots, ignore existing sentencing guidelines, and hand down heavy sentences.

Although these events of the past 30 years or so have shaken the British

LAWS GRIND THE POOR, RICH MEN MAKE THE LAW

establishment to the core at times, the question of a full scale revolution ensuing, that would threaten the establishment's own personal safety, has never been the issue. That is the difference between now and then.

In the 18th century that is exactly what the aristocracy and gentry were afraid of, made even more frightening as they witnessed the events of the French Revolution unfold across the water in 1879. The French church, monarchy and nobility were all obliterated as the French mob took control of the country and turned France into a Republic, not to mention the execution of the King and mass killings of the aristocracy at the guillotines. The fear for the British aristocracy was that the taste for revolution and anarchy would travel across the water and spread like a disease.

The only revolution to have started in Britain at that time, however, was the Industrial one; we had steam, coal, pistons and fire. Although these new exciting technological developments led to many positive and ground breaking changes in Britain, over time, these new forces proved to be equally dangerous for the authorities. They did eventually

become the cause of more riots and bloodshed, giving the lawmakers new and unrivalled challenges.

England, by the end of the 18th century, was going through an enormous transformation. With the Industrial Revolution came invention, ingenuity and lots of new money. In an age of factories, free trade and massive steam engines, Britain was well and truly on the up. There was, however, a downside.

As thousands of people moved to towns to take advantage of the factory work, the population exploded. The living conditions for the workers were pitiful. With labouring wages so very low, people were forced to live in ridiculously cramped conditions and in squalor. It is not surprising, therefore, that disease was also rife. This was perhaps not the best recipe for a quiet, content population where law and order are concerned.

Crime and depravity were spreading like wildfire in these overcrowded towns and cities, and now the fear of being hanged didn't seem to be cutting much ice. Desperate times called for bold measures. The radical idea was then put forward to actually employ people to catch criminals and prevent crime. The idea of having a state run police force had been rejected by the state a century earlier, but it was rejected, partly because they didn't fancy having this new force poking into their own affairs. Also, the similar operations that had been initiated in France using spies and informers had left them cold.

This was, however, a new era and when the establishment saw what was happening to society they changed their attitude towards the idea. As the concept gathered momentum, it caught the imagination of an up-and-coming man in parliament, Robert Peel. In 1829, when he was Home Secretary, he introduced the Metropolitan Police Act. A pretty daring move at the time, yet it resulted in the very first British policemen patrolling the streets of London; it was the world's first professional police force.

The list of duties a new 19th-century policeman had to deal with was just a little different compared with their job today, and included: dog stealing, runaway apprentices, bigamy, furious driving, stealing dead bodies, and pickpockets!

LAWS GRIND THE POOR, RICH MEN MAKE THE LAW

The force originally consisted of 1,000 officers and they were commonly known as 'bobbies' or 'peelers'; they became very much part of everyday life on the streets of London. Their uniform consisted of tunics and top hats, and they were armed with only a rattle. Their principal function appeared to be concerned with keeping a close eye on the working classes so that the gentry would be undisturbed and sleep more soundly at night. Legally, policemen were allowed to apprehend any persons seeming idol, loose or disorderly who they came across lying in any highway, yard or other place, between sunset and eight o'clock in the morning, and who could not give a satisfactory account of themselves.

Today there are over 135,000 police officers in England and Wales alone, and they have extensive powers to arrest and detain suspects, and some are armed. Opinions are divided on whether this should make us feel more secure, or whether it is just a bigger threat to our already compromised civil liberties. It seems that the role of the police, similar to the changes in law making, is and always has been a controversial issue.

The introduction of the police force in the 1800s sent a very clear message to the masses that the rulers were arming themselves with new weapons to enforce law and order. Then of course there was a new problem. What to do with all these criminals once the police officers had apprehended them; even they couldn't hang everyone!

In parallel with the Industrial Revolution, new and enlightened ideas were sweeping across the Continent; these would end up having a direct impact on the law. The great thinkers and philosophers of the time were extremely preoccupied with the ponderings of how to make society a fair and just place for all. They began to challenge traditional customs and superstitions, instead offering a more scientific and rational approach to life.

One of our most radical philosophers was a Mr Jeremy Bentham. As a radical thinker, Bentham was well known for his 'happiness' principle. His idea being that the law should create the greatest happiness for the greatest number of people. In other words, Bentham wanted a representative democracy i.e. the vote. His theory also included getting

RIGHT
Pentonville
Prison 1842.

rid of the monarchy, aristocrats and priests. Although his call for democracy was a little ahead of its time, Bentham did manage to make improvements to the law that would soon bring about a new era of justice. Bentham firmly believed that criminals could be reformed and that it was time to hang up the willy-nilly use of the noose.

Thankfully, Bentham was not alone in his attitude towards hanging and by the 1830s they were not viewed as public forms of entertainment any more, the ruling classes had lost their appetite for them, and they were generally viewed as barbaric. Society required a new form of punishment and Bentham was at the head of that reform.

Due to the evident lack of trust in the law that all the hangings had instilled in the population, it was decided to reserve the death penalty for only the most serious of crimes. Lesser criminals were going to be given the chance to change, so instead of focusing on harming their bodies, the rulers decided to start concentrating on their minds. Naturally, the best way to achieve this was to lock them up.

Although taken for granted today, prisons were a ground breaking new initiative in the 19th century that represented a totally new and enlightened approach to punishment. Pentonville Prison in London was one of the first, and it opened its doors for business in 1842. At the time, the building was regarded architecturally as an icon of its age and it received a huge amount of publicity. Of course, before this, prisoners had only been kept in tiny cells whilst awaiting trial or the death penalty. The concept of actually keeping criminals in cells long term, as part of their punishment, was a totally new and radical idea. It hardly needs pointing out, however, that even though these new buildings were focused on reform, being in a Victorian prison was certainly no holiday camp (unlike some today, many would argue).

The enrolment procedure for all convicted criminals entering an HM Prison involved them being stripped of their possessions and clothes, then bathed in a water bath containing carbolic acid. Their heads were shaved and they were issued with the standard prison uniform. Their name was now a number and they

also had to wear a mask type hat so that prisoners couldn't recognise or communicate with each other. It was frankly all very dehumanising. The idea was that you had to be stripped of everything you had or once were, so that prison could rebuild you.

Reflecting the ethos of the age of the Industrial Revolution, i.e. good hard labour, prison life very much reflected this and this was viewed as the key to reforming convicted criminals into hardworking, moral and upstanding citizens. Although the prisoners were put to hard work during the day, the hours spent in the cells in the evenings alone and in silence drove many mad.

Even though more convicted criminals were locked up rather than executed, the death penalty was still given for the most serious of crimes. The once noisy, crowded and social ritual of the gallows, however, also changed significantly. Any hangings that did take

place were now done behind the closed walls of the prison, and in cold silence.

Hanging may have been abolished, but the idea of keeping criminals behind bars is still very much part of our legal system today. In fact, we hold the European record for locking people up. Even after all these years of this penal system, there is still a great amount of political debate with regard to whether it really works or not. The concept of reforming prisoners and returning them to society as totally changed and moral citizens has not changed in over 170 years. Ironically, the prisons are now more overcrowded than they were in the Victorian era, with cells that were originally designed for one inmate now containing two. The major concern now is that overcrowded prisons simply cannot do their job.

Bentham and his contemporaries were not just concerned with the penal system, their vision encompassed a reform for a better life for every single member of society and believed that using the law was the way to achieve it.

Like many businesses today, factories enjoying the gains to be had from the Industrial Revolution strived for high productivity and high profits. This, however, was very much to the detriment of the workers. Including women and children as young as eight, working conditions were extremely poor, wages were low and days were long for everyone; up to 16 hours for many. The concern about the workers did become a serious issue, but not for any sentimental reasons. The fact was that factories needed fit and healthy workers to keep their productivity high; exhausted workers who dropped down dead were no good for business. For the very first time, the government was about to intervene to address the issue.

The law was put to use in protecting workers from the worst abuses, which in turn would ensure that factories, mills and mines would run smoothly.

Several Factory Acts were passed that restricted working hours, and regulated working conditions. Even parliament seemed to turn into a factory, a law making one. Suddenly everything including trade, transport, education, drink, sex, and marriage were governed by rules. For the railways alone 442 Acts of Parliament were passed over a three-year period.

Even though the general working conditions of the poor had improved,

LEFT
Child Labour.

BELOW
Industrial Revolution Poverty.

they were still very much poverty stricken and living in squalid conditions. Men of wealth were still ruling decisions about their lives, and some began making noises about having the right to vote for themselves. Many were becoming aware that unless the law changed, people in their situation would remain powerless forever. The workers therefore started striking, marching and rioting in an attempt to get their voices heard, and trade unions and workers associations sprang up.

Pretty slow off the mark considering the pressure they were under, in 1832 the government passed the Great Reform Act, but this still left the majority of British people without a voice. As a wave of revolutions swept through the continent in 1848, this time England did not escape its trend, and the workers by this time were very angry, determined and highly organised. Even though so much had changed in England over 100 years, the law hadn't kept up. There was still an enormous gap by the 1840s between those who made the laws and those who had to abide by them. To vote, you had to be an adult, property-owning male, approximately one in seven at the time. The political power was therefore still very much in the hands of the wealthy and privileged few. If the men and women workers wanted laws to be changed that would directly benefit them, then there would

have to be a serious change to the entire political system. The leaders of the day may not have been in much of a hurry, but the working classes were.

With everything that had been brewing over the century so far, the sense of outrage that was growing by the day gave birth to the very first mass movement of the working classes – the Chartists. Rallying behind the People's Charter, they demanded six fundamental reforms, the first of which was the right of every man in the country to a vote. Using the slogan, 'peaceably if we may, forcibly if we must', the pressure they applied on the government was increasing, culminating in a massive rally of 20 to 30,000 Chartists on Kennington Common, understandably making the establishment extremely nervous. It was the biggest political rally in British history.

The main purpose of the rally was to deliver a petition to parliament with over five million signatures. Once the tens of thousands of people had gathered, it became clear that with so many police officers and army present blocking the route to parliament, there was no way they were going to achieve

LEFT
The Great Chartist Meeting on Kennington Common, 1848.

what they had set out to. The Chartists leader, Feargus O'Connor, spoke calmly to the people and told them all to go home quietly, and remarkably they did.

The petition was later delivered to parliament by carriage, but MPs rejected it and instead many Chartist leaders were arrested and imprisoned. The people may have been put away, but their ideas were far too powerful to be brushed aside so flippantly. What the demonstration had shown was that ordinary working class people were absolutely determined to have their say when it came down to the laws of the land they lived and worked in. They would be back to fight another day.

All but one of the six Chartist demands have since become part of English law; the only one missing is the call to have elections annually. None of this happened quickly though, and it wasn't until 1884 when the majority of men got the right to vote. It took another 40 years before democracy, as we regard it today, was finally established, with the final fight being won when women were given the same voting rights as men in 1928.

Bloody Mary

Throughout history there is no doubt that Britain has had its fair share of blood thirsty rulers, yet one in particular stands out from the crowd. This reign was crammed with burnings, tortures and beheadings and more people were executed for their religious beliefs than the Spanish Inquisition did in the same five years. The monarch in question was a woman, and her name was Mary Tudor, who became notoriously called 'Bloody Mary'.

Mary's father, Henry VIII, had dismissed the Catholic religion and turned England into a Protestant country. Her brother Edward VI had also followed in their father's footsteps. But when Mary became Queen in 1553, she had one burning ambition – to turn England back into a Catholic country.

In view of the fact that most of the population were Catholic at heart anyway, the task in theory should have been a fairly simple one. The problem was that Mary took no prisoners, and her methods were so

brutal that by the time she died in 1558, the English people not only hated her, but her religion too.

Although her reign ended so very

LEFT 2011 London Riots.

BELOW Portrait of Sir Thomas Wyatt.

badly, it had in fact started very well, and to begin with the new Queen was extremely popular with her subjects. In February 1554, however, her power was challenged. A gentleman by the name of Thomas Wyatt gathered an army of 7,000 men in the countryside of Kent and marched on London.

Mary had very little time to prepare a defence force, and on the 5th February Wyatt reached the city boundary. When he and his men got there they had terrible trouble crossing the Thames due to the fact that many bridges had been destroyed in anticipation of their arrival. Wyatt spent days frantically trying to find a way to cross the river, by which time most of his men got bored and deserted him.

Eventually Wyatt did manage to cross the river, but by this time he only had 500 men with him. Not surprisingly they now didn't stand a chance against the Queen's army and they were quickly overwhelmed by the troops. Those still alive were carted off to prisons to face trial; Wyatt himself was taken straight to the Tower of London.

Queen Mary had easily crushed the first threat to her throne, but instead of being satisfied with victory, Mary wanted revenge. In the Tower, Wyatt was tortured on the rack so that he would give up the names of his fellow conspirators. Mary was determined to

LEFT Mary and her husband, Philip of Spain.

BELOW Mary in 1544.

hunt down everyone involved in the plot. Despite weeks of torture (and Mary tried everything) Wyatt refused to crack. Mary was convinced that Wyatt's plot had something to do with her Protestant half-sister Elizabeth, later to be Queen Elizabeth I. Wyatt absolutely refused to incriminate Elizabeth, however, so after two months Mary gave up. Wyatt was executed alongside about 100 of his men; most of them were subjected to the horrifying ordeal of being hanged, drawn and quartered. Mary certainly made an example out of Wyatt and his men.

The method of execution hanged, drawn and quartered was arguably the most grotesque in the history of our justice system. The victim would have been cut down from the hanging frame whilst still conscious to ensure that the following part of the torture was felt in full. Next was the castration, a purely symbolic act that visibly cuts off the future bloodline of the tyrant. The disembowelling then commenced: the slitting knife was used to slice the stomach wide open, the entrails were then pulled out by hand and shown to the victim, followed by the liver, and

LEFT Old London Bridge in 1616, with Southwark Cathedral in the foreground. The spiked heads of executed. criminals can be seen above the Southwark gatehouse.

finally the heart. Only at this point would the victim be dead. The head was then cut off and placed on a spike on London Bridge as a warning to all other citizens. The whole process was finished by the quartering of the remaining body, which was dispatched by fast horse rider to where the victim had lived and hung over the city gates. It was therefore clear to everyone what would happen if another plot against Queen Mary were conspired.

The Wyatt rebellion marked a turning point in Mary's reign. After a year of restraint, she suddenly displayed a terrifying ruthlessness. Her treatment of Wyatt and his men was nothing, however, compared with what was to come.

In 1554 Mary married the Catholic Prince Philip of Spain, but now focused all her attention on stamping out heresy once and for all. Being a Protestant, let alone saying anything, could result in various nasty things happening. Having an ear cut off, a hand burnt over a candle, or being given a spell in the stocks for example. Protestants were now regarded as second-class citizens and things

were about to get worse for them.

Mary's need to stamp out the Protestant religion had an added urgency. She had no children, no Catholic heirs, so she was determined to make England as Catholic as she could whilst on the throne. Although for the time her age of 38 was a little late for having a baby of her own, she hadn't given up on the idea. Shortly after the wedding the Queen announced that she was pregnant, but 10 months later, no baby had been born.

Mary was physically and mentally weak, wrinkled, pale and sickly, and was tormented by the thought that the security of her kingdom totally depended on having a child. She tried countless remedies to make herself fit enough to get pregnant. She had uncontrollable fits of temper and her desire for a child was becoming obsessive. In reality, Mary didn't stand a chance of becoming pregnant and this anguish only served to fuel her determination in her campaign against the Protestants.

Mary changed the law after 18 months on the throne that sanctioned

LEFT Cramners Martydom, Burning at Stake.

the burning of heretics. In only four years, 283 met their end via this grisly method of execution, which is on average one victim every five days; England had never seen anything like it.

No one was safe from Mary's purges. Just possessing a copy of the Bible in English meant that you could be burnt alive. Paranoid and terrified people started betraying their neighbours and even their families; the executions took place in town squares all over England.

People were quite used to the concept of being burnt at the stake, as it had been a practice that was 150 years old, and it was also a social day out! The moment the flames were lit, everyone would jostle to get a better view and the best seats were naturally reserved for the town's most important folk. One of the great ironies of this method was the tradition of a bag of gunpowder being hung around the victim's neck. Often given by family members, the idea behind this was to help make the death quicker and less painful. Unfortunately what the people didn't know is that gunpowder needs to be put in some kind of hard container to actually do damage.

Just tied around the victim's neck, it would ignite and blow a little, but would only have charred the person's head and neck, in fact adding to the pain and suffering of the victim.

The Bishop of Gloucester, John w, was the first high profile heretic that Mary sent to the stake and 7,000 people gathered to watch his horrific death. Not enough wood was used to create a good fire, so the Bishop had a very slow and painful death. It wasn't, however, just important figures like the Bishop that were being killed like this, it was happening to everyone from farmers to hat makers.

Mary couldn't understand why her message wasn't getting through to the people; they all seemed to be prepared to die for their beliefs. The more people burned, the more sympathy was shown to the victims. She did, however, have a final trick up her sleeve that she hoped would scare her people into submission; she had a prisoner, the former Archbishop of Canterbury, Thomas Cranmer. Cranmer, having served Henry VIII, had been the brain behind turning England Protestant.

Having already watched the horrific

LEFT
John Hooper.

deaths of many of his contemporaries burn from his cell window in the City of Oxford, Cranmer abandoned his faith and turned Catholic. Normally, this would have been acceptable, but he was dealing with Queen Mary, who absolutely despised him. Bloody Mary burnt him anyway in 1556.

Being used to seeing heretics burnt at the stake was one thing, but the English people had never seen such important people executed in this way, and had certainly never seen persecution on such a scale. Some protested at the burnings and at church services; the people were beginning to turn against their Queen.

Mary was seeing both of her dreams die rapidly – turning England back to Catholic, and having a baby to secure its future. As her health, both physical and mental, deteriorated she ordered the burnings to continue. She was still signing death warrants on her own deathbed. In just four years, Mary had burnt more people than had been burnt in the previous 150 altogether. Mary died on 17th November 1558, and with her death came the death of this horrific and bloody period in history.

The Witchfinder General

In the 1600s, England was awash with blood as the Civil War ripped the country apart. Away from the battlefields, another war was going on; a terrifying and sinister war that killed more than 1,000 innocent people in 200 years. This was the war against witches. The area where the witch hunt was the most vicious was in East Anglia, where 200 witches were hanged in a period of 18 months.

Up until 1614 most witches were imprisoned, but that was all about to change. In East Anglia one man was single-handedly determined to rid the country of the devil and his witches for good. This grim episode began in the Essex villages of Manningtree and Mistley where this one man caused panic, paranoia and mass hysteria.

His name was Matthew Hopkins and between 1645 and 1647 he caused the death of at least 200 witches, most

of them women. One would now call him a serial killer, but he preferred to be called the Witchfinder General. The son of a clergyman, Hopkins was a religious fanatic, and his mission was to rid society of all enemies of God. He appeared on the scene at the perfect time to start a witch hunt; the 1640s saw civil war, death, disease, poverty and crop failure, and people were paranoid.

The belief was that such misfortune could only be caused by the devil whose evil agents were at work throughout the land, and witches got the blame. The country was in upheaval, not only in politics, but religion too. The monarchy had gone and with it the last vestiges of Catholicism, which included all the religious traditions that helped protect the average person from the devil, the power of the priest and exorcism for example.

The Protestants had different ideas. The church couldn't save you from the devil and his witches; you had to deal with that yourself. No longer having religion to protect them, therefore, the villagers became extremely paranoid. Prior to having the witchfinders to help them, they relied on all kinds of mumbo jumbo and strange rituals to ward off evil. Witches couldn't be identified just by looking at them, so if they got too close it would be too late.

Despite all the potions and charms, the people were still paranoid. The

only way to solve the problem was to identify them and put them to death. Hopkins was the ideal man to hunt them down and string them up.

He was an educated and shrewd man, having also been legally trained, he knew the law very well and therefore how to get around it. In fact when he started his witch-hunting career the total chaos in England meant that there weren't any rules to go by and crucially, no one to judge him. The fact that Hopkins didn't have any official authority didn't even cross the minds of the paranoid villagers; they gladly ran to him with all the gossip and rumours.

Conveniently situated as the landlord of the local pub, The Thorn Inn in Mistley, Hopkins was in the perfect place to listen to and gather local information. With villagers spreading rumours about other villagers, hysteria was rife. Nobody could be trusted, friends and relatives included.

The victims of the accusations were always easy targets: the weak, the helpless and the old. Hopkins' very first victim was an 80-year-old widow with one leg, Elizabeth Clarke. Having lived in the village all her life, her age and disability

only strengthened the case against her. She was stripped, shaved and searched, as they wanted to find the mark of the devil on her body as proof that she was a witch. Known as 'familiars', creatures of the devil (often thought to take the shape of an animal) were thought to have fed off the witches' blood. Any strange marks, blemishes, or even moles would have been viewed as proof. If a mark was found, the witch was pricked and if she didn't bleed or feel pain, then she was in cahoots with the devil. Crafty witchfinders would have used trick knives for example, where the blade moves up the handle even though it looks like the knife is going into the body; therefore no pain and no blood. Not surprisingly Hopkins found a mark on his first victim and Elizabeth Clarke was branded a witch.

Once identified, witches were taken away for further interrogation, an interesting use of the word rather than torture, as Hopkins fully knew, torture was illegal. For Hopkins this took the form of sleep deprivation and psychological torture. After four days and nights without sleep Elizabeth confessed to being a witch. She was

LEFT Execution of alleged witches, 1587

then pressed into naming others, which she did. This continued as captured and accused women started pointing the finger at others; the witch hunt was beginning to grow very nicely indeed for Hopkins. No one was safe. Daughters blamed mothers and

neighbours turned on neighbours as paranoia made people bring down others in an attempt to save themselves.

By 1645, the interrogation of Elizabeth Clarke had directly led to the arrest of 36 others. As Hopkins' reputation grew so did his eagerness and within four months he had made himself indispensable. The local Colchester prison was filling to the brim with interrogated and tortured witches awaiting trial. In order to keep up the hysteria and hatred for witches, every so often they were taken out of their cells to be abused by the locals, who would heckle them and throw things at them. They were kept like this for a few months before being carted off to courts to be tried.

Hopkins' real aim was to have these women tried and killed, but issuing the death penalty was the job of the court. In 1645 he got his wish, however, and 36 women were sentenced to hanging. Not only did Hopkins have an easy job, he was also well paid for it, earning £1.00 from the local magistrate for every witch hanged. Not surprisingly as his power and ambition grew, so did his death toll as he moved from Essex into neighbouring Suffolk and Norfolk as well.

By this time Hopkins needed a more public verification of witchcraft and along came the new form of publicly witnessed interrogation – the ducking method. By throwing a witch in water, if she floated then she must have supernatural powers and if she sank she's obviously innocent, albeit dead. Hopkins used every trick in the book to ensure that his victims floated.

By 1646 the Witchfinder General had arrested hundreds of witches and most had hanged for their forcibly confessed sins. One particular elderly priest he managed to get a confession out of and hanged was, however, a step too far. People thought that he was getting out of control and got suspicious about the validity of his work. By autumn of 1646, one man was ready to call his bluff. The Reverend John Gaule decided to put an end to Hopkins' work. As his witch death toll was approaching 200, Hopkins was beginning to feel the heat of the law on his back. Rumours and complaints about him eventually reached parliament.

Hopkins was a cunning man and not a fool, however, and disappeared from the witch-hunting scene before anyone could catch him. Without him around whipping up hysteria, the witch hunts went cold. The fate of Matthew Hopkins remains shrouded in mystery and myth.

LEFT
Colchester Prison.

The Monmouth Rebellion

The last battle to be fought on English soil was the Battle of Sedgemoor, which was a gruesome gun battle fought at night between the forces of King James II and the ordinary men who fought alongside the Duke of Monmouth. This was the climax of one of the bloodiest events in English history – the Monmouth Rebellion.

The South West of England rose up in a desperate attempt to overthrow a much-hated king. The scenes of the battlefield left enough strewn bodies and blood, but when the actual battle was over, the killing did not stop there.

The Monmouth Rebellion did not have anything to do with Wales; it all took place in the South West of England. As with most bloody feuds of our history, this too was bound up with religion.

In 1685 England was mostly Protestant, but the new King James II was Catholic and his subjects wanted to get rid of him, and their chance came just four months into his reign. On 11th June 1685 a mysterious ship appeared just off the Dorset coast at Lyme Regis. Aboard was the Duke of Monmouth, the bastard son of the late King Charles II and nephew to King James. His intention was to kick his uncle off the throne. The people of England were ripe for rebellion as the Duke began gathering his supporters. King James, however, had been notified of his nephew's arrival to England and his intentions.

With nearly 1,000 raw recruits after three days in the country, Monmouth needed to turn the rabble into a credible fighting force that could face the army of the King. Unfortunately the fighting equipment available to them was not quite to the same standard as their enemy would have, not to mention

ABOVE
Battle of
Sedgemoor
Memorial,
Attribution
Rog Frost.

the lack of body armour. This event is also known as the 'pitchfork rebellion', for this very reason. They did have muskets but these took 35 seconds to reload after each shot; Monmouth's men didn't have long to master the art of loading and firing them.

Heading out of Lyme Regis,

Monmouth went from town to town and his campaign was fast gathering momentum. The only problem was, he didn't really have a clear plan of action. He marched his troops haphazardly around the West Country and wouldn't attack any royal strongholds. Three weeks into

the rebellion, he was encamped at Bridgewater surrounded by demoralised and exhausted men; thousands deserted him. Whilst Monmouth dithered, the King's army were only just outside the town on the fields of Sedgemoor, and preparing to strike.

On the afternoon of 6th July 1685, Monmouth received word that the Royal Army was camped just three and a half miles away. He climbed the spire of Saint Mary's church in Bridgewater to survey his enemy. To his delight, he saw that they were clumsily arranged and that their infantry and guns were vulnerable. Monmouth decided that he would attack and that he'd do it in the dead of night.

Those who remained loyal to Monmouth silently marched toward the army at 11 p.m. The rebels outnumbered the Royal Army by about 600 men and of course a major advantage was that they didn't know the rebels were coming. About a mile and quarter from their enemy the silence was, however, broken as a shot was either mistakenly fired or done on purpose with an insider amongst them. Either way, the rebels had been rumbled.

Monmouth first sent forward his cavalry under the leadership of Lord Grey. 600 men on horseback charged towards the King's army, but they didn't get very far. Coming across a ditch, instead of seeing if they could get over it, Lord Grey ordered the cavalry to turn right to find a bridge to cross. It was a disastrous decision as the horses galloped directly into the enemy firing line. Grey panicked and the cavalry fled, but even worse, they ran straight through their own infantry causing utter chaos.

Monmouth had now lost his two advantages: surprise and superior numbers. He rallied his remaining men and they advanced and reached a ditch; at 2 a.m. they opened fire. A vicious gun battle ensued as the two sides pounded each other in the darkness with gunfire for an hour and a half. The dreadful realisation then dawned on the rebels that they were running out of ammunition.

At dawn the royal cavalry crossed the ditch and surrounded the rebels on three sides. Monmouth and his surviving men only had one way to run and that was backwards. It was, however, during the morning of 6th July, with the

THE MONMOUTH REBELLION

RIGHT
King James II.

FAR RIGHT
Monmouth's
execution on
Tower Hill, 15
July 1685.

few miles from the coast they were arrested. The once famous and flamboyant Monmouth was hardly recognisable; he was thin, unshaven and shabbily dressed. In this miserable state he was taken to the Tower of London and King James gave the order to behead his nephew swiftly. The execution of a Duke was a massive event and the masses flocked to watch it. On 16th July 1685 the Duke of Monmouth was beheaded at Tower Hill, although it was a very messy affair as the executioner did not have a good day and it took him several attempts to do the job.

Even though Monmouth's beheading was not a good example, a beheading was a privilege reserved for the nobility, as it was supposed to be quick. The rest of the rebels who had been systematically hunted down were in store for something much worse.

Battle of Sedgemoor over, that the real slaughter took place. The rebels were chased down, pulled out of trees and hiding places and ruthlessly massacred by the royal troops. 1,384 rebels died that day, compared with only 50 of the King's men. Those who did manage to escape that massacre may have wished they hadn't, as the King's revenge to come was even more barbaric.

Monmouth and Lord Grey had left the battlefield early and were heading for the nearest port, in disguise. Just a

Thousands of the surviving rebels were caught and locked up in makeshift prisons, such as churches and town halls. Often a few were hanged from the trees outside, their dangling corpses left to rot. The following actions of King James were savage, even by the standard of those times.

The Royal Army's killing spree came to an end seven weeks after the Battle of Sedgemoor, when King James sent his top judge to the West Country to hear the rebels' cases in a proper court. It was the now infamous, sadistic Judge Jefferies who got the job. The concept of fairness was an alien one to Jefferies and although a Protestant himself, he was driven by personal ambition. Rather than administering justice, he saw it as his duty to champion the King's cause, and his trials became known as the 'Bloody Assizes'.

With 1,500 cases to hear, Jeffries announced that those who pleaded guilty would be shown mercy, which meant that he could pass sentence without having to hear any defence evidence; a very clever trick. Judge Jefferies travelled to the various towns in the West Country and took just nine days to try all 1,500 rebels. 330 of whom were executed, most of these were hanged, drawn and quartered, and 849 were transported. From then on Judge Jeffries name became synonymous with bloody justice.

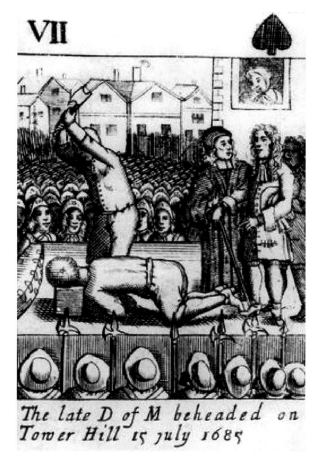

The late D of M beheaded on Tower Hill 15 July 1685

The pictures in this book were provided courtesy of the following:

WIKIMEDIA COMMONS
www.commons.wikimedia.org

Published by: DEMAND MEDIA LIMITED & G2 ENTERTAINMENT LIMITED

Publishers: JASON FENWICK & JULES GAMMOND

Written by: **MICHELLE BRACHET**